Get Real, Get Recruited!

Get Real, Get Recruited!

by Treva Farmer

Foreword by Randy Moss

This book is dedicated to the subject of this writing, the ones who inspire me daily - the children.

I am also inspired by my parents, Arthur and Beatrice Farmer. They taught me to see the end from the beginning and showed me what enduring love, unwavering commitment a 58-year marriage looked like.

Thirdly, my grandmother Pauline Lucas impacted me in a major way. She marched to her own beat and refused to allow her past to dictate her future.

Get Real, Get Recruited!
Position Yourself for a Chance at College Sports

Table of Contents

Foreword

Coming from Rand, West Virginia, a place most people have never heard of, school, church and sports were about all we had to do. I guess because we didn't have most of the distractions kids have today - texts, tweets, Instagram, and all those kinds of things - my friends and I became good at whatever sport we pursued.

I've played sports all my life - football, basketball, baseball and track, but had I known there was a process for getting recruited, I am sure I would have made some better choices. My mother did what she knew to do; however, had she been better informed, we would have focused more on the important things that go into making the right decisions about college and sports.

Don't get me wrong. Marshall University, my alma mater, was good to me, and my professional career has opened many doors. However, in spite of all the money that changes hands in college athletics, what matters at the end of the day is how well prepared you are to recognize and go after opportunities.

In my ongoing quest to help young athletes in the community, l recently coached at a small school my son, Thaddeus, attended. While there, I met Treva Farmer, a counselor who asked me to read a book she had written to help students who want to be recruited.

Although she doesn't come across as your typical sports enthusiast, she has connected with a variety of coaches and players who have poured information into her that she wants to pour into you. She cares enough for you to show you the other side of recruiting… the students' and the parents' side.

After reading "Get Real, Get Recruited!," I agree this is a must read. It doesn't matter if you are a five-star athlete or if you are unranked, Division I, II or III, you can benefit from the information contained in this book.

You will learn things such as:

- Why student athletes need parental support more than anything else
- How to get noticed by colleges and universities
- How to tell when a college is actually interested in you
- The importance of knowing your level of talent
- What to do if you have already messed up in high school
- The types of questions you should ask to avoid missing out or making wrong decisions.

What you are lacking, many times, has nothing to do with your athletic ability. Usually, it's a lack of knowledge that stands between you and the right opportunity. Athletes have to achieve in the classroom to earn the privilege to play. So I encourage parents and student athletes, to set aside time to read "Get Real, Get Recruited!"

It's an easy read, so it shouldn't take you too long to finish. But take your time, digest a couple of chapters at a time and then discuss them as a family, so you can develop the right game plan for <u>you</u>. Since recruiting is big business, and the rules are constantly changing for the NCAA and other athletic associations, let's stay on top of how the game is played.

Keep in mind your college choices should not center around parties and social life, famous athletes you want to hang around, or staying close to friends. It's about identifying where <u>you</u> are, knowing how to prepare yourself and pursuing every available opportunity to make your dreams come true. So, get busy and start reading!

- Randy Moss

Introduction

Welcome to Get Real, Get Recruited! I provide guidance to high school athletes on the academic and compliance side of recruiting. As a school counselor, part of my job is helping young men and women successfully transition to college level sports. Young people and sports are two huge passions in my life, so this part of my work is especially fun.

On many Sundays or games days, you can find me glued to a television, watching every play of a basketball or football game, so don't try to hold conversations with me until halftime, please. And yes, hometown loyalty is big with me, win or lose. So, go Panthers and Hornets!

What began as a guide for our school's athletes to use on official visits has blossomed into the book I am excited about sharing to assist athletes everywhere. My purpose comes purely from a desire to help prepare athletes for one of the biggest decisions of their lives.

I don't have to be a national recruiter, a sports analyst or a hall of famer to connect with children on the heart level and see in their eyes a burning desire to become the best athletes they can be. But most don't know how to get there.

My inspiration to write this book comes largely from my grandmother, who was a remarkable woman.

Polly, as she was affectionately called, gave birth to my mother at the age of 17 during a time when it was more than shameful to have a child out of wedlock. So she started out against the odds. Because of the situation she found herself in, her mother sent her down the road to work full time at Fort Bragg, the military base nearby. Unable to spend much time with her young daughter, Polly relied primarily on her mother to bring her up.

Yet, she was determined not to allow her past to dictate her future. Eleven years later she married and subsequently bore four more children. She became well respected in her community because of her perseverance through difficult situations, her love for people and her delicious sweet potato pies! Grandma went on to earn her GED at age 75. As a member of the local senior citizen's group, she won over 50 Senior Games medals in her latter years and retired her bowling ball in her early 90's.

Grandma and I were the hard-core sports duo. If there were a game on television, we were usually right there on the sofa, cheering our teams to victory!

Her true loyalty, however, was to the Chicago Bulls, led at that time by Michael Jordan. At the height of Jordan's career when she was probably in her late 70's, someone bought her a Bulls Starter jacket. She couldn't wait to wear it when I took her to a Bulls/Hornets game in Charlotte. That's when the original Hornets were one of the hottest teams in the league.

Amidst a sea of Hornets' teal and purple, she strutted proudly into the Charlotte Coliseum adorned in her red and white jacket. Of course, Jordan literally tore us apart that night. But I'll never forget the sheer excitement I saw on her face as she experienced her first and only professional sporting event and witnessed the skillful dismantling of our home team.

Grandma finally transitioned from this life in 2013 at age 101. These precious memories have continued to fuel my passion for sports over the years—and my determination to never give up.

Athletic recruiting is a very intriguing business. Between watching college and professional athletes' careers evolve over the years, talking with many college coaches and helping high school athletes navigate through the eligibility process, I have learned a great deal. Since playing sports on the collegiate level is a dream for so many, I'd like to help demystify the recruiting process and hopefully save you time and from making major blunders.

There is so much to know about getting recruited, but I will share with you what I have learned and what I believe will help you most. Hopefully after gaining some insight into what it takes, you can determine if moving to the next level is the best move for <u>you</u>.

I say this because playing on the college level is more than a notion. If you are going to make a difference on your team and position yourself for the next level, if that's what you want, you'll be making much more of a commitment than you ever imagined. Here's a hint: For the most part, your days will no longer be yours. Your nights will no longer be yours. It'll be like a fraternity or sorority, and your coach will be your Dean of Pledges. That's just the way it goes. But more about that later.

Treat this book like you would 'insider information' on how to buy a car. An overwhelming majority is unaware of the right way to do it and become easy prey for skilled salespersons. Just think how much time and money we could save if we knew the ins and outs of buying a car and could cut through all the fluff and negotiations!

I would like to thank God for the gift of passion for writing. Also, special thanks to Dr. Robyn Gool, Michael Pratt, Randy Moss, Dee Brown, Kourtnei Brown, Joseph Johnson, Dr. Janet Miranda, Sporty Jeralds, Leah Metcalf, Kenya McBee, Ramona Patterson, Kory McNair, Tiara Cloud, Cheryl Drew, Lacy Farmer, Tisha England and Cary Mitchell for their contributions to this book.

1

Attention Parents: They Need You

If you are going to allow your children to play sports, they need and deserve your full support. Here is what I mean by support:

A. <u>No work, no play</u> - Simply put, your children will not qualify to play sports on the next level if they fail to perform adequately in the classroom. Extracurricular activities are provided to enhance and extend student learning and experiences beyond the classroom. They build character, teamwork and time management skills while helping students prioritize and develop their gifts, talents and people skills. They also help children with making long-term commitments. Sports activities are optional privileges in the high school equation and secondary to academics.

To help children prioritize as they mature so they can earn and keep these privileges, it is wise to set your own family expectations in academics and behavior and stick to them. Understanding priorities early will help them develop the character they need to be successful as adults.

Read the story of Patrick Peterson, cornerback for the Arizona Cardinals. Peterson's sophomore year in high school, his parents kept him out of football for a season because his grades had begun to slip because he was cutting classes with his friends. Not only did they keep him out, they even required him to watch his teammates play while he was sidelined. What a great life lesson!

As a result, because of the discipline and tremendous work ethic he developed after returning, Peterson is now among the highest paid cornerbacks in the NFL. Student athletes are called student athletes for a reason.

To what extent will you go to help ensure your child's success? Some may argue keeping their children out of sports hurts the team. Well, let me ask you this: which would you rather "hurt," the team, or your child? Would you really put winning ahead of your child's well being? Sure, many coaches step in and assume a parent's role when necessary by applying "tough love." But should they bear the weight of that responsibility if you are visible and actively involved in their lives?

B. Hard work? What's that? - Along these same lines, children do not come out of the womb understanding the value of a strong work ethic. They have to be taught. I have heard parents say, "I told him to do his homework," but did you do regular checks to see if he was producing quality work, and did you locate the proper resources if he was struggling?

In sports, as well as the classroom and in life, children need specific instructions, a routine, accountability, and the right kind of help to develop their talents.

They need to know how to handle frustrations, push through in hard times and to delay their gratification. Coaches teach this in large part, but the foundation should come from home, because the primary responsibility does rest with you! This very important quality will distinguish the athletes who will likely play on the next level from those who may not get the chance.

C. Manners, please - Colleges invest millions of dollars in their athletic programs, and coaches don't have time for disrespectful, self-serving athletes. In most cases, their jobs are on the line, and they are unwilling to risk their careers or their programs on undisciplined, underperforming, high-maintenance athletes. Sure a few players slip through because their larger-than-life profiles translate into big dollars for the university. But generally speaking, there are too many eager, talented and qualified athletes out there who want to do it right for colleges to settle for anything less. So please, hold your children accountable for behaving properly. Don't enable irresponsible behavior. It will likely hurt their chances of moving forward and cause both of you a lot of frustration, embarrassment and heartache. Teach them that following guidelines at home and in school is just dress rehearsal for the next level….and for life.

D. <u>Show up, but don't show out</u> - Many children leave it all on the court or on the field or maybe never even get in the game, but when they look around for the most influential persons in their lives, where are you? Any child who works hard to achieve, in the classroom or in sports, craves the approval and support of their parents. Do other obligations always seem more important than being at the game? Do you often overlook opportunities to compliment what your children do right and instead just nitpick and criticize their performance?

Are you there only when their names go up in lights and the media is swarming around them, or are you their biggest fan when they are struggling? They need to know you are with them through the good and the bad times, so please show up, and please don't embarrass them when you do. They need to see you as reliable support.

E. <u>Work with the coaches</u> - Just like any other human being, coaches are not perfect, so give them your support as they work to develop your child's talent. However, one thing I don't advise is tolerating abusive treatment from coaches. The key is recognizing the difference between abuse and structure (discipline). Encourage your children to always do their best and show respect, and they will likely receive it in return.

2

Be realistic about your level of talent, grades and scores.

Guys and girls, please don't mistake desire for talent. Just because your Uncle Mike who played quarterback two years in college convinced you and your parents you are league material does not mean you are. Oops, did I just say that? Really, you would be a lot better off getting an unbiased opinion from someone who knows.

To play college sports, you've got to have talent, grades and scores (SAT/ACT) — the entire package. So, get real by finding out what your true talent level is, what it's really going to take to get where you need to be to qualify, and then go do it! You'll pay the price if you want it badly enough.

Remember, college sports are for those who are stronger, faster—those who are plain 'puttin' out' on the high school level, not for those who just play well when recruiters come around or when their future is on the line. You've got to distinguish yourself from others around you one way or another. You've got to stand out!

However, even if you don't possess these qualities, you may still have the mentality, fundamentals and the toughness to play in college. It is important to honestly assess your strengths and weaknesses and seek the level best for you. Keep in mind that even if you don't land a Division I scholarship professional scouts seek talent on all levels.

All too often, I have counseled athletes who looked me seriously in the eyes and shared plans of playing football at schools like Auburn, for example, with a 1.6 grade point average and a SAT score of 550 (Critical Reading and Math combined). Trust me, this is not a match. It just will not happen without a 180-degree turnaround.

Also, it's possible to meet NCAA or NAIA qualifications and still not meet the college's minimum GPA requirements for admission. Colleges do not base their entrance requirements on athletic scales. They have their own set of criteria, so I would advise you to find out the requirements on both ends.

Am I Better at Football or Soccer?

Secondly, do you know which sport you are best at? Which one do you seem to have a better or natural ability for? If your 40 time is 4.4 and your agility is very good, but you are a 5'5" 150-pound running back, you'd probably be better off developing your footwork and talents in soccer rather than football (or honestly seeking an opportunity in a division other than Division I). No "offense" intended, but you'd get smushed to a pancake in about 4.4 seconds on a Division I football field! Remember how Wile E. Coyote looked after he was flattened by a truck on the old Roadrunner cartoons? You might enjoy a better life with a cushy white ball between you and the ground instead of a 300-pound defensive tackle on your back!

However, I realize there are always exceptions to the rule. If you are a great deal smaller than the typical athlete who plays your position, but you are a tenacious competitor with an unusual amount of skill, speed and heart, like Muggsy Bogues or Steve Smith, you could possibly get noticed. That's the beauty of determination.

While you are getting real, though, watch out for the advice you may get from your friends. If you want to play college sports, the guy who rarely does his school work, shows up late for practices and puts forth a half-hearted effort on the court or field can't help you. Neither can the cousin who squandered his athletic talent in high school, and now while chugging a can of beer talks only about what he coulda, woulda or shoulda done.

Talk to your coaches, parents, counselors and teachers to find out what <u>you</u> need to do physically and academically and then get busy! This is not just a suggestion, but a critical step toward being ready when it counts!

Ideally you want to be sure you are on track no later than ninth grade and stay on track so you don't have to change negative habits or play catch-up. That's generally when your academic achievement starts to be recorded on your transcript. Also, athletic recruiters who are looking at upperclassmen can get an early glimpse of your talents if you have begun to excel in sports early.

In short, it is very important that you surround yourself with positive people — those who have your best interest at heart, will tell you the real truth and will push you to be your best.

A word about natural gifts and talents: Here is a good way to gauge whether or not you are cut out for college sports. Do a self-check. Rate yourself from one to 10. If you're a natural six who, with a strong work ethic could easily develop into an eight or nine, then you could possibly gain the attention of college coaches who are willing to put money on the line for you and work with you. On the other hand, if you have made some contributions on the high school level but are a solid three performer who has to work extremely hard to get to a five, you might consider developing your talents in areas other than sports. The key is being honest with yourself.

What to Do If You've Already Bumped Your Head

Let's say you messed up early in high school, and it's going to take a miracle to get that serious look from the Division I program you're dreaming about. If you don't find your name on their roster after National Signing Day and you are still not close to qualifying, the question becomes, "Are you willing to humble yourself, go to juco (junior college), get your grades up and then transfer?" Junior college, sometimes referred to as community college, is a smart alternative to prepare you for a four-year college, even if you're not trying to qualify to play sports. And, contrary to what many believe, it is not a last resort for those who weren't able to go anywhere else.

After improving your grades and successfully completing the required credit hours to transfer, then you can apply to the four-year school you originally wanted to attend. Your high school coaches are invested in your success. Ask them to help you locate a junior college athletic program that has a relationship with a four-year institution that will transition you into their university. I have heard many football and basketball television commentators introduce stars on Saturday afternoon as junior college transfers. Who cares how you got there?

Eligibility requirements are getting tougher, which is reason to stay ahead of the game, rather than just barely qualifying or missing the mark.

3

Find Out What Coaches Look For

Aside from speed, strength, good grades/scores and good manners, coaches are looking for athletes who know the fundamentals of the game or those who are teachable. They want those with good field or court sense, physical abilities and mental toughness to compete at the collegiate level. Can you overcome adversity and persevere during tough times? Do you understand what it takes to win? Are you a team player .... or are you all about self?

"What type of player are you when adversity strikes?"

- Randy Moss,
Retired NFL wide receiver

Generally, the higher the division (Division I being the highest), the more skilled you have to be.

On that note, let me say a little about Divisions. There are three National Collegiate Athletic Association (NCAA) Divisions: I, II and III. The divisions are distinguished based on the number of varsity sports, collegiate sponsorships, team schedules, game attendance and other factors.

Division I schools are generally the largest and overall have the highest level of financial backing. They're the ones you regularly see on television, although some Division II games are also televised. Division I schools offer full athletic scholarships. Division II offers grants combined with financial aid, and Division III does not offer athletic scholarships. Then, there is the National Association of Intercollegiate Athletics (NAIA), a separate athletic governing body, which also offers scholarships. The NAIA is divided into Divisions I and II. Thirdly, there is the National Junior College Athletic Association (NJCAA), which governs junior college athletics.

To play for an NCAA Division I or II school, you must register for and be determined eligible by the (NCAA) Clearinghouse. The Clearinghouse is just what its name says —it is the national governing body that clears student athletes to play college sports. They determine if you can successfully handle the rigors of academics while playing sports by comparing your core course grade point average with your college entrance test scores (SAT or ACT) to establish eligibility. This is why academic performance in high school is so important.

What is a core course?

A course that qualifies for high school graduation in one or more of the following: English, mathematics, natural or physical science, social science, foreign language or comparative religion or philosophy;
* Is considered four-year college preparatory;
* Is taught at or above the high school's regular academic level;
* For mathematics courses, is at the level of Algebra I or higher; and
* Is taught by a qualified instructor as defined by the appropriate academic authority.
* No remedial courses are allowed.

Ask your athletic director or counselor to compute your core grade point average so you will know where you stand.

These days, I am convinced many toddlers' first words are "DI." They all want to play for DI schools! Impressionable young athletes are often mesmerized by the notoriety and name recognition of these institutions, so they overlook opportunities at other schools that may be a better fit. Children cut their teeth on these names and can easily be distracted by their popularity. Take my home state, North Carolina, for example. There are a number of very strong Division I programs here. I grew up watching ACC basketball and was confused about why any athlete would want to play in any other conference!

You can find strong programs, skilled athletes, highly-qualified coaching staffs and state-of-the art facilities in all divisions, in every part of the country and on every level of play. Again, you will determine where you land based on your qualifications, available opportunities and marketability. So, by all means, consider <u>all</u> of your options.

If, after reviewing all the possibilities you decide to only consider Division I offers, please realize you may be limiting yourself to becoming just a practice player on that level as opposed to getting significant playing time and development at a Division II school. That's the real.

A 2013-2014 study of U. S. high school athletes by <u>scholarshipstats.com</u> revealed a little over 7% (about one in 14) went on to play a varsity sport in college, and about 2% of high school athletes (one in 50) made it to the NCAA Division I level. Although these statistics are low, you still have a good chance of making it into that 7 or 2 percent if you maximize your skills, get the right kind of information and use it properly.

<u>Also, contrary to what some may believe, character does matter.</u> Since most coaches' careers rise and fall on their win/loss records, they treat coaching as a business and for the most part have no time to baby-sit. Therefore, your conduct means more than you probably think. I encourage you to read John Maxwell's *Talent is Never Enough*. In this book, Maxwell outlines 13 key choices that can be made to maximize any person's talent. One of the key choices is protecting your character.

A coach of a very popular Division I school called me a few months ago for a character reference on one of our student athletes. He said part of their recruiting process is interviewing a school official outside the athletic department to learn more about the character of potential recruits. Fortunately, I was able to give him an excellent reference on the young man. Please conduct yourselves in a manner in which people will always have something good to say about you.

4

Understand the Recruiting Process

A. Market Yourself -

This is still a free country. Before any coach reaches out to you, your first plan of action should be to develop and implement your own marketing plan. If for some reason no one shows serious interest in you, does that mean you are not talented? Of course not. It's inexpensive, convenient and easy to effectively promote yourself through the Internet and social media.

First, build a portfolio of your talents with quality game highlight film, stats, GPA, an athletic resume and athletic recommendations. If you really want to distinguish yourself, build a website which highlights your game film and stats. Then develop a list of schools you might consider attending and review the NCAA schedule to determine when you can start sending your portfolio to them. Take advantage of online services like Facebook and Twitter and make your film available through sports-related media outlets. <u>But please use these online tools wisely!</u> Recruiting coaches review these sites regularly. Immaturity can cause you to post inappropriate material, so please use discretion in your postings.

"The use of social media in recruiting is vital these days in the exposure of the athlete, but you must understand how to use it properly and the dangers of pressing 'send'."

- Dee Brown
Retired NFL running back

Also, be willing to participate in summer camps colleges host. This is a great opportunity to showcase your talent, and you can possibly get your name on their recruiting list if you excel.

B. Letters and E-mails

If you hear from a recruiting coach by letter or e-mail, it is likely they got your name from a database, a questionnaire you completed or from your personal contact with them. This type of correspondence goes out to hundreds, perhaps thousands of players each year and does not necessarily mean the school wants you to sign with them. But go ahead and actively pursue the ones you are interested in. To distinguish yourself from the rest and keep all your options open, show courtesy by responding to all of them, by phone call or e-mail, thanking them for their interest in you. On pages 27-30 of the ***NCAA Guide for the College-Bound Student-Athlete*** (found on the NCAA website), you will find guidelines on when and how you may contact coaches, as well as when they can contact you.

C. Transcripts

If a college coach contacts your school for your transcript, there is a possible interest. They are filtering out prospects based on grades, scores and performance. Take the initiative to follow up with the appropriate person at your school (counselor or registrar) to be sure they respond to recruiters in a timely manner and provide the information they requested. Hopefully coaches will see your best effort on paper, because depending on how good your grades look, that could determine if you go any further in the process.

D. High School Campus or In-Home Visit

By the time college coaches visit you at your high school or in your home, it is clear they are interested in the possibility of your joining their roster. At this point, they have usually already seen your film and know your stats, so they are coming to learn more about you personally and find out how you might fit into their program.

An important note about visits: When a coach takes the time to visit you, whether in your home or at school, always show courtesy and respect even if you're not interested in the school. Realize your seventh choice today could become your first tomorrow.

All too often athletes get the "big head" and decide they don't have time to talk with a Division II coach who stops by to see them, because they are only interested in playing in a Division I program. Well, what happens if you don't qualify to play Division I or your name suddenly drops from their recruiting board and you've disrespected all the DII coaches who showed a serious interest in you? You're up the creek, dude! A coach's commitment to you is not set in stone until you sign the papers. Please be aware that your status can change overnight, because coaches rearrange and re-prioritize their order of recruits throughout the entire recruiting process.

More importantly, coaches have a network; they talk to each other about their potential recruits because they are all after the same thing—the best player for the position. So, if you burn your bridges with one coach, the news will travel quickly through the coaching ranks. Be mature and again, keep all your options open.

Thirdly, when recruiters come to visit, they want to hear how you have done your best to maximize your academic and athletic potential, not a rehearsal on what the coaches, counselors or teachers are not doing for you.

As a student athlete, you should know where you stand academically. You should also complete college entrance testing (SAT/ACT) and register for the Clearinghouse by the end of your 11th grade year. Your being prepared in these areas indicates to coaches that you have taken responsibility for your future. It causes you to look more like the "total package." It will also eliminate what I call the 'big sweat' during your senior year. That's when college application deadlines and recruiting coaches are suddenly staring you in the face, and you don't have the grades or scores you need. Here are some tips for successful recruiting visits:

➢ Know the recruiting/visit schedule (pages 27-30 in the Guide). Coaches know when they can visit and when they can only call (or text and tweet). Make sure you know also. But also pay close attention to and avoid prohibited activities which may be construed as recruiting violations. Violations can include such things as receiving gifts or educational expenses from coaches. You and your parents are responsible for knowing what's acceptable and what's not.

➢ Whether the meeting occurs in your school or at another location, realize you should be as curious about their program as they are about you. So, don't hesitate to ask questions. There is no need to feel like you're being interviewed at this point. Relax.

➢ Although they understand you are a teenager, coaches appreciate students who communicate well—those who are assertive, articulate and deliberate in their conversations. So be sure to make good eye contact and greet them with a firm handshake.

➣ Your attitude should be one of gratitude because of their interest in you, but don't become starry-eyed—you are competing against other prospects for the same position. In addition to being professionals, coaches are also skilled salespeople who are on a mission to sign the best prospects for their programs. To help you keep visits in perspective, remember the attention you are getting now is short-lived.

➣ Once you sign with a school, things will become business as usual, and they will expect you to fall into the ranks and get with the program! And keep this in mind—the scholarship you sign for is only a one-year contract. Although most scholarships are renewed for the traditional four years, coaches still re-evaluate their players each year based on performance, team needs and new recruits to decide if they want to renew individual player's scholarships.

"Whether you are on an unofficial, official or in-home visit, don't fall for all the hype. Selling their image and showing you their best is the school's objective. But once you arrive at the school you choose, it'll be like going into the workplace, which won't be as glamorous. Your coaches then become your new bosses."

-Leah Metcalf, U. S. Professional
Basketball Player, Europe

➢   Meetings should always be conducted with a representative from the school present, i.e., coach, other athletic department representative, or school counselor or, if you're at home a parent, to ensure all discussions are above board and your interests as a minor are protected. If one is not in place, discuss a school protocol with administration or your athletic department to establish how much time you should spend at the meeting table with a coach. It is important to monitor this, especially if you are a highly-recruited athlete. Too much time out of the classroom can cause you to fall behind in your school work. Coaches should not be allowed to spend huge chunks of time with you during the school day, because after a certain point it can turn into excessive marketing.

➢   Be sure you understand the questions you are being asked. If you are not sure, don't hesitate to restate the question or ask for clarity. At the same time, be ready with several basic questions of your own, such as:

1. Explain your academic support system for athletes. Are tutors and mentors involved in this process? How many times per week am I required to attend tutoring and study hall sessions?

2. Would you tell me about your position needs and the guys/girls who will play in front of me?

3. How competitive are your practices and schedule? How often will we watch film?

4. Who is your head coach, and for how long is he under contract? Who would my position coach be? What is his history and experience?

   A list of other questions you can ask when you arrive on campus will be given later in the book.

Many college coaches and school officials offer perks to pressure highly-recruited athletes and their parents into signing with their schools. Sometimes they offer monetary or material incentives or alter grades for athletes who don't qualify -- whatever it takes. So, tell me, who's the real winner?

Depending on the situation, your decision could land you and the school you choose sanctions, disqualifications and maybe even a trip home! It's good to be excited about an opportunity most athletes won't get to experience, but you and your family must approach this process soberly as well, or else you could end up losing. Think carefully about every decision you make so your story can be one of success rather than tragedy.

Here's the short on recruiting: In football, for example, a staff might send 10,000 to 15,000 letters and watch 1,000 to 2,000 videos before making 500 phone calls to potential recruits, verbally offering between 65 and 200 scholarships and extending up to 85 offers for official visits before signing a maximum of 25 players per year!

5

Choose Specific Colleges to Visit

Unofficial visits, visits for which you pay your own travel expenses, can take place any time during your junior or senior year and are unlimited, according to NCAA rules. You can actually use these visits to narrow your choices.

However, during official visits, colleges pay for your transportation, food and lodging in most cases. These visits must take place during a specific period of time, depending on the sport. In football, for example, visits start in January each year and are followed by an official signing day which is the first Wednesday in February.

Official visits may last no longer than 48 hours and can occur only during your senior year in high school. During these visits, you should receive official tours, speak with coaches, players and other people affiliated with the program, and you may stay overnight on campus.

Because you are limited to a maximum of five (5) visits, make the most of each official visit and focus only on the schools you can see yourself attending. Take into consideration the following questions as you are narrowing your choices:

> ➤ Does the school support or facilitate an atmosphere to help you grow in the way you have been brought up, or is it neutral or indifferent to your needs?
> ➤ Are you comfortable with the size of the student body?
> ➤ Is the school close enough to home or far enough away from home? (Ask yourself, "How easily could I adjust to a school far away from home?") Does the school offer programs to support you if the distance from home is significant?
> ➤ With that in mind, in case of a family emergency, how quickly would you be able to get home?
> ➤ If considerable distance is involved, are adequate resources available for you to go home on holidays and special occasions?
> ➤ Does the school offer your major?
> ➤ Can you adjust to the urban, suburban or rural environment of the school?
> ➤ Can you enhance your athletic skills with this school's program, or will you become stagnate based on the level of skill and competition?

Never choose a school based on a head coach or a position coach. Coaches leave all the time for more money and to climb the ladder, or because they've been fired. Secondly, never allow a relationship (girlfriend or boyfriend) to determine where you go either! What happens if the two of you break up in the first month and you discover he or she wasn't your life partner after all? <u>Here is a rule of thumb: If you were not playing sports at this school, would it still be a match for you?</u>

6

Prepare Before the Official Visit

A.   Dress for success! Be sure to dress your best for your visit(s). If you have not done so, invest in a good black or gray suit and tie. Consider saving your orange suit for signing day. By then, you're in and, although it may not appeal to the masses, you can get away with doing your own thing.

Making a favorable impression can go a long way and will further distinguish you from the rest. You can dress down in appropriate casual attire at the appropriate time during your visit. Be sure your hair and nails are well groomed. And please, no drooping, guys or girls!

B.   As the day of your visit gets close, if you have not heard from your contact person at the school, call ahead to confirm.

C.   Make a list of questions you would like answers to. Carry a portfolio of some type, or this book so you can keep your list handy and record your answers. (Note pages are included at the end of the book for your convenience). You may have received answers to many of your questions during the coaches' visits to your school or during your campus tour. However, be sure to get answers to the following questions before making your final decision:

Team

> You are already a nationally-recognized team. What part can I play to make your school look even better?
> What are your short-term and long-term goals for your team?
> How do you plan to accomplish these goals?
> What was your record this year?
> What resources are available in your athletic department to help me maximize my talent?
> Tell me about your strength and conditioning program—where does it rank compared to the other schools I'm considering, and what do you specialize in?

Academic

> What was your team grade point average this year?
> What percentage of your players graduate? How often are these statistics re-evaluated?
> Of the players who go pro before graduating, what percentage ultimately return to graduate?
> Explain your tutorial/mentoring program for athletes.

➢ How do you handle practices that conflict with my class schedule? Do the professors work with the athletes in these cases? How?

➢ What portion of tuition, books and fees are covered by this scholarship offer?

➢ Does the scholarship cover summer school if I need to attend?

➢ What types of degrees have your players graduated with, and what percentage of them become gainfully employed or enroll in graduate school?

➢ What commitment do you and your staff have to seeing that I graduate?

➢ If I have to remain in school a fifth year, would the scholarship cover this?

➢ What happens to my scholarship if I am injured?

Spiritual & Family Needs

➢ What type of relationships do you have with former players and their families?

➢ If there is an emergency at home, would I be able to go?

➢ Do you have a team chaplain? What programs are available to help enhance my spiritual growth during my time here? (i.e., FCA, Athletes in Action, Campus Crusade for Christ, Team Bible study, church affiliations, etc.)

➢ Is there a list of area churches available to me? Will I have the opportunity to attend church on Sundays?

Campus and Community

➤   What kind of support do you receive from the student body and from the community?

➤   What is your crime rate on campus and in the local community?

➤   College football and basketball players are often featured on the news for breaking the law off the field. How does your staff educate athletes to keep them out of trouble, and what kind of curfews are imposed?

➤   Have any of your athletes gotten into major trouble? If so, how did you handle it? If not, how would you handle it?

➤   Explain the athletes' living arrangements. Would we live in dorms or apartments?

➤   Are athletes housed with other students, or separately?

7

The Official Visit

Colleges are highly skilled at marketing their athletic programs and dazzling young high school athletes. So, if you have experienced game day festivities in the locker room during your official visit or on the playing field during an unofficial visit, you may get 'hooked' well ahead of Signing Day.

That's right….the music, the screaming fans, the videos and even the jerseys with your name on them can "reel you in" before you even know what hit you! And don't take a run through the tunnel with the team, or you're probably hooked for sure by then. How could you <u>not</u> see yourself there?

This plan works for many. "I can't explain how good it felt for me to be there," said one national recruit. "They played the whole tunnel-walk thing for us and gave us jerseys to wear out on the field. Just hearing my name and being able to run onto a college field like that was great. That's when I made my decision."

Get Real, Get Recruited!

Although you may ultimately end up choosing this school, don't fall in love so fast! Remember, you've got five visits. Your final choice of schools should be one that meets all the objectives you and your family established at the onset of your search.

The real psychology behind it all requires that you have the ability to separate your emotions from reality and know who you are. By keeping the right perspective, you can remain level-headed and grounded in your decisions and end up in the place best for you. That's all the more reason you should be totally prepared for the official visit.

On to the visit…..

Think of your campus visit like a trip to your local car dealership. While you can surely buy a car without seeing it and checking it out first, you'll probably make a wiser purchase if you get behind the wheel and take it for a test drive.

<u>During your campus visit, it is critical to ask a lot of questions and do a lot of active listening</u>. Be sure to speak with the following people to get all the pertinent information you will need to understand who you will be working with:

> Admissions Officers – To be sure you fully understand the school's admissions requirements and process
> Financial Aid Officers – Even if you are on scholarship, you may also be required to

40

apply for federal student aid. You and your family need to understand what is expected of you in this process and exactly what you need to do to secure monies you might be eligible for each year.

➤ Academic Advisor - This person will be a VIP in your life and will help you stay on track with your academic requirements! Find out this person's expectations and the kind of help available to you. Ask him or her questions like, "How can I get the class I need that's offered at night and doesn't fit into my schedule," or "Can I major in what I want to major in and still play this sport?" Ask this person to give you an honest and candid roadmap of your academic plan.

➤ Faculty in your area of study – Meet the instructors who will be teaching you (and make it a point to develop good relationships with them once you are enrolled).

➤ Students – Be friendly. Other students can tell you a great deal about the atmosphere of the school and the athletic department.

➤ Student-athletes – It is important to observe those you'll be playing with to get a sense of how happy they are. Observe the attitudes and overall morale of the players. If you have the opportunity to spend the night with a potential teammate, don't hesitate to get the inside scoop! Do plenty of listening and observing!

> Team spiritual leader – A good way to learn about the spiritual state of the team. Find out what his/her goals for the team are.
> Athletic Director – This person is your head coach's boss. Find out his/her philosophy and outlook for the team.
> Sports Information Director – This is the person who will make you look good to the school and to the public.

Make sure you visit the housing and academic facilities since so much of your time would be spent there. Take note of the special resources and services available to athletes, such as computers, tutors or mentors. Notice if student life there seems to offer a healthy balance between classes, studying, social events and extracurricular activities.

<u>And finally, please realize the official visit *is* your interview</u>! This is not the time to wild out or grab every carrot placed in front of you. Coaches are watching to see how much you will drink and party and if you will fall for the woman or man used as bait. They want to see how you handle distractions because that will indicate how you will conduct yourself as a member of the team. If you think I'm joking, just ask some recruits whose offers were rescinded <u>after</u> the official visit!

"Will your academic major set you up for a successful life after sports? What true preparation and life skills will you get in exchange for your athletic abilities? Know your worth!"

-Kenya McBee,
Former U. S. Professional
Basketball Player, Europe

8

Offer or No Offer? - Show Me the Papers!

By the time you are done with official visit(s), if you were presented at least one offer, your head might be spinning from the excitement over the possibilities! You're probably wondering where to go, what to do. At this point, it is critical that you clearly define what you were told during your visits. Coaches are weighing their options heavily, and you should be too. They are evaluating and prioritizing recruits and making their final selections.

Although you may have received a verbal offer from a college during your junior or senior year or during an official visit, you still should not view the school's commitment to you as money in the bank until you receive the scholarship documents in hand. In other words, show me the papers!

If you're a quarterback, for example, a typical college has probably offered you and three other recruits the same scholarship, because they don't know which one of you is going to accept. They're counting on their number one pick to take the offer, but guess what? You may or may not be their numero uno! So, get real and know exactly where you stand with their offer before you start making decisions!

Offers can come in the form of full athletic scholarships or they can be a combination of grants-in-aid and financial aid. The bottom line is <u>before you make a commitment to any school, ask them to provide you with a written offer</u>! Written offers are usually distributed a few days to a week before National Signing Day. All too often athletes make commitments to schools before receiving the papers in hand and don't realize until they have rejected other offers that the one they accepted is not what they thought it was.

Once a school makes a commitment to you, this contractual agreement, once signed, should be honored. Unfortunately, this does not always happen.

Take the case of Jeremy B. (fictitious name). Jeremy was recruited by several Division I schools. A highly-sought-after running back, he was plagued with borderline grades. Recruiters followed him his entire senior year but slowly dropped off, one by one….except for one school that made him an offer at the end. He pushed hard and qualified to play right before graduation, only to have his scholarship revoked by the school a month or so later when a new head coach decided he would require a higher academic standard. The contract should have been honored as a legal and binding agreement, but this school got away with that one! (I still have the documents in my files.)

Or how about Howard R.? Howard weighed the benefits of offers he received from two Division II schools and ultimately chose the one he saw as the better offer. But because he made his decision before receiving his Letter of Intent, when he contacted the school to secure the paperwork, he learned the full scholarship had been given to another athlete and all they had left for him was less than $3,000 per year. Apparently, while he was busy deciding, he did not know his stock was going down. The coaches had decided to go another route. In the meantime, the school he had declined gave a much larger award, which had been earmarked for him, to another athlete. As a result, Howard was left with the smaller offer. True stories!

Also, some offers are conditional and can be rescinded if you fail to uphold your end of the agreement you make with a school, so stay focused and finish strong!

Please realize, ladies and gentlemen, recruiting is a business, sometimes a cold, hard business, and must be treated that way from beginning to end.

What Color is Your Shirt?

Finally, before you accept an offer, get more specifics about the team's plans for you. You must get coaches' answers to the hard questions ahead of time. As I mentioned earlier, you should know if you will play immediately, or if you will be "redshirted". A redshirt athlete practices with his team and can even dress for play but does not travel or compete with the team for one year. He or she has four years of eligibility remaining after the first year, however, and is eligible for scholarship monies the entire time.

Players are generally redshirted for two reasons: 1) to allow more time for them to develop physically, mentally, emotionally or academically and 2) for the school to solidify position depth for the future while current athletes on the roster complete their years of eligibility.

Athletes can also be greyshirted. This term is used to designate a high school athlete who delays their initial enrollment in a college. The athlete, usually in NCAA Division I football, doesn't enroll in college the fall after high school graduation, but delays enrollment until the spring semester.

This usually occurs when a university doesn't want to consider the football athlete to be an "initial counter" (freshman scholarship offer) until the following academic year because they've already reached the limit on scholarships they can offer.

Another reason athletes are greyshirted is to postpone the start of their five-year eligibility clock.

The blueshirt status is basically the same as a greyshirt with one significant difference. Whereas a greyshirt shirt athlete delays enrollment at the university until spring, the blueshirt enrolls in the fall and plays as a walk-on without a scholarship for at least the first semester.

This allows them to participate in practices and perhaps even play in games as true freshmen and receive scholarships later on. As walk-ons, they are not counted until the following academic year.

And, finally, there's the greenshirt athlete. The term used mostly in football, but increasingly more in soccer and volleyball, refers to athletes who graduate from high school a semester early to enroll in college and begin practicing with the team in the spring. They learn the plays, train with their team and bond with teammates before the fall season.

No matter what color shirt you accept, make sure you understand your status and restrictions <u>before</u> you sign so you can make an intelligent decision.

9

9

Voices - What Are You Hearing?

Once you and your family, or those responsible for your well being, have obtained sufficient information and begun to narrow your choices, who you listen to is critical. Don't be deceived by all the voices you'll hear urging you to, "go here," or "go there." Although some will be genuine, some will not be, and you've got to know the difference. This is a good time to narrow your circle of influence.

Ask yourself these questions:

- Does the person(s) advising me have ties of any kind with the recruiting college, and is he/she possibly steering me to a particular school for personal gain?

- Does this person attempt to exert an unusual amount of control over me and my family's decisions without regard for my preferences?

• Has he or she failed to make me aware of recruiters' attempts to contact or visit me?

Just make sure you know which channel to tune your radio to - who you should tune in, and who you should tune out - so you can have a fair chance at making the best decision for <u>you</u>.

"You're the one who will be going to that university for four or five years. Coaches have their reasons for wanting you there, and families have their reasons for wanting you at a certain school. But at the end of the day, you have to be happy about the choice you make. Would you be happy there if you're not playing football?"

-Kourtnei Brown, DE/LB
Tampa Bay Buccaneers

Conclusion

Remember, aside from offering you a great athletic experience, college is an opportunity to explore your interests, uncover hidden talents, challenge your weaknesses, discover your passions, develop autonomy as an adult and grow spiritually. Hopefully, it will help build stronger character and strengthen your work ethic that will propel you to success in professional sports or another career.

If you earn the privilege to play sports in college, good for you! After you have done your homework about the recruitment process, you should have peace about the decision you and your parents make. When you know you're in the right place, it will be much easier to handle the challenges that will arise. So get real, and get recruited!

"Get Real, Get Recruited! is a 'get real' book that not only communicates with players, parents and coaches, but it connects. Now that you have read the book and you know better, you must do better!"

- Coach Tisha England,

Newton Conover High School Hall of Fame, Catawba County, NC Hall of Fame, NAIA Women's Hall of Fame, USC-Aiken Hall of Fame

Appendix
College Visit Log (Key Points to Remember)

University 1	Recruiting Coach	Position Coach	Date Visited

Likes:

_____

_____

_____

_____

Dislikes:

_____

_____

_____

_____

Questions I need answers to before I commit: (possible deal maker or deal breaker):

_____

_____

University 2	Recruiting Coach	Position Coach	Date Visited

Likes:

_____

_____

_____

_____

Dislikes:

_____

_____

_____

Questions I need answers to before I commit: (possible deal maker or deal breaker):

_____

_____

_____

University 3	Recruiting Coach	Position Coach	Date Visited

Likes:

_____

_____

_____

_____

Dislikes:

_____

_____

_____

_____

Questions I need answers to before I commit: (possible deal maker or deal breaker):

_____

_____

_____

University 4	Recruiting Coach	Position Coach	Date Visited

Likes:

_____

_____

_____

_____

Dislikes:

_____

_____

_____

Questions I need answers to before I commit: (possible deal maker or deal breaker):

_____

_____

_____

University 5	Recruiting Coach	Position Coach	Date Visited

Likes:

_____

_____

_____

_____

Dislikes:

_____

_____

_____

Questions I need answers to before I commit: (possible deal maker or deal breaker):

_____

_____

_____

For more information or to get your copy of
Get Real, Get Recruited!, contact us at
NewEaglepress.com.

www.ingramcontent.com/pod-product-compliance
Lightning Source LLC
Chambersburg PA
CBHW061509040426
42450CB00008B/1535